FIFTY STATES, NOT SIX

A Bipartisan Approach to Reforming
the Electoral College and Assuring that
Every Citizen's Vote Counts

James W. Lucas

ISBN-13: 978-1544219820

ISBN-10: 1544219822

Constitution Renewal Initiative

www.TimelyRenewed.com

cover by StudioBridger

TABLE OF CONTENTS

TRIGGER WARNING: This book may contain information which could be *disturbing, even traumatizing, to some readers.* For example, if you are a Democrat looking for a screed denouncing the deplorable Republicans for opposing direct popular election of our president. Or if you are a Republican looking for a diatribe decrying the perfidious Democrats for opposing the Framers' perfect scheme for electing our president.

However, if you are an American who:

• is curious how we came by our current system of electing the President
• is open to considering a proposal to improve that system that accommodates all sides, and
• is in favor of every citizen's vote counting in selecting all of our Nation's leaders, in Congress as well as the presidency,

then this short book may be of interest and use to you.

ONE

Picking a President –
What the Electoral Colleges Were Supposed to be
vs. What They Are

The video appeared on YouTube shortly before Election Day in November 2012. A little girl, probably around three years old, was crying in her car seat. One hears an indistinct voice on the car radio as her mother asks "what's the matter Abby?" Her voice breaking with the despair that only a three year-old could bring to an encounter with the underside of the adult world she was coming to know, Abby cries "I'm tired of hearing about Mitt Romney and Bronco Obama!" Her mother is then heard assuring her that it would all be over in a few days, after the election.

Abby's tragedy was that she was a resident of Colorado (hence her version of the sitting President's name). Had Abby lived to the north in Wyoming, to the west in Utah, or to the east in Kansas, she would have been spared the assault of harsh-sounding political ads. If she lived in New York where I live, or in our most populous state, California, she might not have even known there was a presidential election going on.

But Abby lived in what was considered a "swing" state in the 2012 election. Because it was thought that there was a possibility that a plurality of Coloradans might vote either way in the presidential election, they were bombarded with advertising from both campaigns. While this was distressing to those with young Abby's sensibilities, it also meant that the campaigns paid close attention to whatever issues they thought were of concern to citizens of the Centennial State.

However, no such attention was paid to most of Colorado's neighboring states, thought to be intractably Republican, or to New York or California, thought to be immutably Democrat. Our Constitution provides that the president is chosen, not by direct election, but by the votes of electors chosen in each state. The number of electors is equal to a state's representation in Congress, with each state thus having at least three electors corresponding to two Senators and the guaranteed minimum of one member of the House of Representatives. Since the House of Representatives is apportioned by population (an issue to be discussed later in this book), more populous states have more Representatives, and hence more presidential electors.

All but two of our states (Maine and Nebraska are the exceptions) have decided that all of their electors will vote for the winner of a plurality of the overall popular vote in that state. Thus, even in a close election, the winner gets all of that state's electoral votes, negating the voice of all of the other voters in the state. For example, in the most recent election, Donald Trump carried Michigan by only 10,000 votes, receiving only 47.3% of the popular vote. However, he received all 16 of Michigan's electoral votes. The votes of the 52.7% of Michiganders who voted for Hillary Clinton and other presidential candidates (such as Libertarian Gary Johnson or Green Jill Stein) were zeroed out.

Because of this winner-takes-all system, states which are thought to be solidly in one camp or the other are ignored. Instead our modern presidential elections tend to focus on, and be decided by, only a few "swing" states. These perhaps six or so swing states (the "six" states of the title of this book) thus hold vastly disproportionate influence on the choice of who will be our president.

Also, in case you haven't heard, in the most recent presidential election Donald Trump won the majority of votes in the Electoral College s even though Hillary Clinton received millions more votes. This is the fifth time the candidate with the most popular votes has lost the presidential election in our history (the others were the elections of 1824, 1876, 1888 and 2000). This has outraged Democrats, who have come up short in every one of these five cases. As we will discuss later, this disconnect between the Electoral College and popular votes is also largely a result of the winner-takes-all policy.

This book presents a proposed constitutional amendment called the "Popular Electoral Vote Amendment" which will reform the Electoral College system so that every citizen's vote counts.

What the Electoral Colleges Were Supposed to Be

You may well ask why the framers of our Constitution set up such an oddball system, where in every election a few swing states decide the outcome, and occasionally the winner of the poplar vote even loses.

The answer is simple. The way the Electoral Colleges work today is <u>not</u> what the framers of the Constitution intended. Here a bit of historical perspective is helpful. When the constitutional convention met in Philadelphia in the summer of 1787, its delegates represented a nation spread over vast distances. Most of the population was rural, and communication by horse or sail from one end of the country to the other could take weeks. Some modern critics of the Electoral College system portray it as a conspiracy by the elite to block the people from voting directly for the president. However, direct popular election was never an option. The initial assumption at the Constitutional Convention was not that the president would be elected directly, but rather that he would be elected by Congress.

The reasons were practical, not conspiratorial. Everyone knew George Washington, and that he would be the first president. But after him, how would voters know about possible presidents from other parts of the country? There were no national newspapers or organizations to spread such information. To put it in a more recent context, how would voters in rural Georgia learn about a fine young senator from Massachusetts named John Kennedy who might be a good president, and how would voters in rural Massachusetts learn anything about a talented governor of Georgia named Jimmy Carter? The idea of the Electoral Colleges was conceived by a delegate from Pennsylvania named James Wilson, not to block popular participation in presidential elections, but rather to facilitate it. Voters would elect well-informed local people who they knew and trusted, and these would meet, learn about, and decide among possible national leaders. These one-time electors would much more closely reflect local views than members of Congress (who were, and still are, barred from being electors.)

Initially there was no expectation or rule that a state's electors vote unanimously for one candidate. They were supposed to exercise independent consideration and judgment. This old conception of electors was recently revived when many Democrat celebrities and others tried to persuade electors from states carried by Donald Trump to nonetheless vote for someone else. (Ultimately only two Trump electors voted for someone else, compared to five Clinton electors.)

What the Electoral Colleges Became, and Why They Continued

These efforts were doomed because of a development which transformed the Electoral College system within our Nation's first decades. This was the rise of political parties. The Constitution's framers abhorred the idea of political parties, or 'faction' as they called them, but parties appeared even before George Washington left office, and have dominated American politics ever since. Electors thereafter ceased being independent actors, but rather became representatives of the political parties. Aided by advances in printing technology, the political parties provided organized ways of spreading information throughout the Nation about presidential candidates. And to maximize their take of electoral votes, the dominant political parties in the state legislatures passed laws providing that the winner in the state's voting received all of the state's electoral votes. (Indeed, sometimes in the early decades the majority party in some states' legislatures selected the electors without bothering with a popular vote.) The Electoral Colleges ceased being the deliberative bodies they were intended to be. Instead they became simply a rubber stamp formality in this party controlled winner-takes-all system.

Despite the fact that the Electoral Colleges no longer functioned as intended, the system persisted because it helped implement significant aspects of the original Constitutional system. In our era of powerful presidencies, it is easy to forget that, in the original constitutional system, Congress was seen as the pre-eminent body of government. This view had an important history. In 1689 in Britain, the Glorious Revolution established that the elected legislature was to be the supreme political power, not the monarch. Today almost every nation in the world maintains at least the form of an elected legislature as the supreme form of legitimate government, and the British parliament is rightly known as the "mother of parliaments."

Thus, it was with good precedent when, a century later, the mini-parliaments which had been set up in each of the British North American colonies decided that they had a right to tax themselves, and ultimately declare their independence. And when representatives of those legislatures met in 1787, just short of the centennial of the Glorious Revolution, to establish a new national government, the biggest issue was how the new national Congress would be constituted.

1. *The Electoral College system helped effect the three-fifths compromise.* It was accepted that the House of Representatives would somehow reflect the different sizes of the states. But how was that to be

measured? While slavery was legal in all of the states (it was not until the early 1800s that northern states began to abolish it) the large majority of slaves were in the southern states. The northern states argued that representation in the House should correspond to the number of free citizens in a state, but the southern states wanted to count their slaves. The solution was the notorious "three-fifths" compromise, which counted each slave as three-fifths of a person in allocating how many seats a state would have in the House of Representatives. Because the number of votes a state's Electoral College could cast was based on its representation in Congress, the three-fifths rule gave citizens in states with large slave populations more Electoral College clout than citizens in states with few slaves.

As a result of the three-fifths compromise, the Constitution was written to base representation on states' total population, not on the number of citizen voters in the states. Chapter 3 will discuss how the Popular Electoral Vote Amendment will end this carry-over of the three-fifths compromise.

Some modern critics of the Electoral College system tend to merge it with the three-fifths compromise. However, technically the two are separate. After all, slavery was abolished 150 years ago, but the Electoral College system has continued to function. Nonetheless, its role in translating the three-fifths compromise into power in the election of the president undoubtedly played a role in keeping the system in place, even after the Electoral Colleges had changed into rubber stamps run by the political parties. (Perhaps unsurprisingly, a majority of our presidents up to the Civil War were slave-owners.)

2.   *The Electoral College system helps effect the big state / small state compromise.* Fortunately, the three-fifths compromise mostly disappeared with the end of slavery. However, another major compromise struck at the Constitutional Convention remains with us.

Then, as now, there were large disparities in populations between larger and smaller states. The compromise was to give every state two Senators regardless of population, while allocating seats in the House of Representatives on the basis of population. (Note again that, because of the three-fifths compromise, the allocation of seats is based on a state's total population rather than its number of citizens.)

This flows through to the Electoral College since a state's allocation of electoral votes is based on its total representation in both the Senate and House. This gives less populous states a little boost since even the least populous states get two electoral votes corresponding to their two Senators. This compromise was based on the less populous states' fear that the national government would be dominated by the more populous states, including their domination of presidential elections. With the Electoral College system, there is a cap on how much more populous states can influence the election, and candidates have an incentive to pay attention to less populous states because of their two "bonus" electoral votes corresponding to their two Senate seats.

Benefits of the Electoral College System, After All

This aspect of the Electoral College is much criticized by direct popular vote advocates, who often are academics from more populous states. However, there are small "c" constitutional and other considerations that underlie giving this modest assist to less populous states:

Many less populous states are Democrat. Democrats from populous states argue that this small small state advantage benefits more rural conservative states. However, this ignores the fact that four of out ten least populous states are reliably Democrat (Hawaii, Rhode Island, Delaware and Vermont, and in presidential races the District of Columbia). Highly regarded leaders of the Democratic Party, such as

Joe Biden and Bernie Sanders, hail from these states, not to mention Hawaii-born Barack Obama.

Giving less powerful regions some electoral advantage is the norm for democratic nations. In the United Kingdom, for example, England is the 800 pound gorilla in terms of wealth and population. However, it has 20% fewer seats in Parliament in proportion to its population than Scotland, Wales and Northern Ireland. The constitutions of Canada, Australia and New Zealand all explicitly allow variations in the populations of election districts to favor rural areas. France and Japan have variations between their most populous and least populous election districts on an order of three-to-one.

Vast power differences divide regions of the United States. These democratic nations recognize that political power is more complex than reflected by a rigid, simplistic, one-person one-vote formula. One would have to be living in a bubble to not recognize the enormous cultural and political influence of New York and California, with their complete control of the Manhattan and Hollywood based media, news, arts and entertainment industries. The few extra votes accorded to states in "flyover" country by the Electoral College system only marginally offset the tremendously disparate power and influence wielded by the coastal elites in our society and politics.

<u>*The Electoral College system disfavors sectional candidates.*</u> Because the populations of China and India are so enormous, we often do not pay much attention to the fact that the United States is the third most populous nation in the world. We are also arguably the most diverse nation in the world. The peoples of no other nation display such racial, religious, ethnic and regional cultural diversity. Unfortunately, this diversity has not always yielded unity. As much as 3% of the Nation's population died in the Civil War. The equivalent in today's population would be over seven million dead.

While no one foresees another civil war, our sectional divisions are obvious. This can be seen from a map of county-by-county election results. The middle of the country largely glows Republican red, with blue Democrat fringes hugging the Atlantic and Pacific coasts. Without the state-by-state voting required by the Electoral College system, with caps on electoral votes moderated by the small two-vote bonus for less populous states, candidates would focus on driving up their gross vote totals in their areas of strength. Presidential campaigns would become regionalized, and the Nation's divisions would grow as candidates abandoned the expense of nation-wide outreach.

The potential for such divisions is illustrated by the most recent election. Hillary Clinton's popular vote margin over Donald Trump appears to have been approximately 2.8 million votes. This difference can be entirely attributed to her 4.3 million vote margin of victory in California. In other words, Donald Trump won the popular vote by almost 1.5 million votes in the other 49 states. Now one can well argue that Californians are Americans too, and their votes should count. However, what would happen to our national sense of unity if the rest of the United States came to see the choice of president as dictated by one single state? It was precisely to avoid such divisive scenarios that the Constitution's framers set up a system with a few features like the Electoral Colleges to provide a little protection for states which were less powerful and less populous.

Obviously, the Electoral College system does not prevent campaigns from stressing their regions of strength. The South is going to be largely Republican and New England largely Democrat (the opposite of a century ago). And the winner-takes-all rules seriously distort elections by narrowing campaigns to a few swing states. But if we set aside the effects of winner-takes-all, the Electoral College system forces presidential campaigns to be more national, and avoid relying on regional strength as would happen with a national direct popular vote.

A decentralized state-based voting system with whole electoral votes reduces disruption from recounts and election fraud. Many readers may recall the chaos which surrounded the 2000 presidential election, where a voting recount in Broward County in Florida kept the Nation in suspense for weeks until the U.S. Supreme Court finally called a halt to it. In the event of another close race, a direct popular vote system would turn the entire Nation into Broward County, as recounts could be demanded in every one of the Nations' thousands of counties and election precincts.

Direct popular election of the president would also be vulnerable to small, hard-to-detect voter fraud across many election precincts. Up until recently, election fraud had become a bitter partisan issue, with Republicans claiming that it is widespread and Democrats arguing that it is minimal. Democrats would point out that there are relatively few prosecutions for election fraud. Republicans would respond that most election fraud occurs in predominantly Democrat jurisdictions, where Democrat prosecutors and election bureaucrats are unlikely to attack their own party's election-rigging.

However, this argument has shifted since the most recent election. Disclosure of extensive hacking, perhaps by foreign powers, has led many Democrats to wonder if there was tampering with election system computers. Although to date there is no evidence of this, there is now general agreement that, in our heavily computer-dependent age, tampering with election computers is a real risk. Focusing the presidential election to 538 electoral votes tends to wash out the effects of small errors and fraud. Each electoral vote corresponds to hundreds of thousands of votes, so there has to be a lot of voting mistakes or major cheating to swing one electoral vote. Big errors and fraud are easier to detect, and thus prevent. Of course, as we saw in 2000 in Florida, all these benefits of the Electoral College system are lost where winner-takes-all rules apply.

TWO

Don't Abolish the Electoral College, Fix It:
The Popular Electoral Vote Amendment Part I

Is there a way to keep the advantages of the Electoral College system while aligning its results more closely with the popular vote? The answer is *yes*. The Popular Electoral Vote Amendment consists of two basic elements, both of which are needed to truly align our national government with the choice of its citizens. (The full text of the Amendment is in the Appendix to this book.) In summary, the two elements are:

• continue allocating electoral votes based on states' representation in Congress, but end winner-takes-all and have states allocate their electoral votes in proportion to the popular vote in that state; and

• eliminate the last vestige of the three-fifths compromise by basing the allocation of seats in the House of Representatives and their corresponding electoral votes on the number of citizens in a state rather than its gross total population.

This chapter will review the first element, proportional allocation of electoral votes, and the next chapter will examine aligning citizenship with the right to choose our national leaders.

The problems with the Electoral College system are not inherent in the system, but rather come from the practice of giving all of each state's electoral votes to the winner of a plurality of the state's popular vote, even if that candidate gets less than a majority. As we saw in the last chapter, these winner-takes-all rules were not how the Constitution's framers intended the Electoral College system to work. They are not required by the Constitution, and were only introduced by dominant political parties to grab the most power for themselves in presidential elections. They effectively disenfranchise many, and sometimes most, of each state's voters, and distort presidential elections by leading them to focus on only a few swing states. Therefore, the first element of reforming the presidential elections system is to eliminate the winner-takes-all rules.

Proportional Allocation of Electoral Votes

The best way to bring the presidential election system more into alignment with the popular vote, while preserving the unifying and protective function of giving less populous states a small offset vis-à-vis powerful populous states, is to keep electoral votes, but have the states allocate their electoral votes proportionately.

To start with a simplified example, suppose a state has five electoral votes and its popular vote in a presidential election is 60% for Candidate A and 40% for Candidate B. Under the proposed system, Candidate A would receive three electoral votes and Candidate B would receive two, instead of Candidate A getting all five. The views of all the state's voters would be reflected in the national totals of electoral votes.

This small change would transform our presidential elections. Since presidential candidates would have the possibility of gaining electoral votes even in states dominated by the opposite party, they would be powerfully motivated to run truly nation-wide 50-state campaigns, rather than focusing on a few swing states. Because less populous states would still have their two "bonus" electoral votes, the campaigns would not ignore them as they would with a direct popular vote system. The change would affect individual voters as well. It would now make sense for liberals in Texas and Wyoming and conservatives in California and Vermont to vote and engage in presidential elections. Overall turnout would increase, and our democracy would become much healthier and robust.

To streamline matters more, we would eliminate the actual electing of individual electors and their formal meeting in Electoral Colleges in each state to vote for President. This would align the system with how elections actually function in our times. It would also remove the possibility of rogue 'faithless' electors who can vote contrary to the will of their fellow state citizens who elected them.

Advantages of Keeping Votes Whole

With electoral votes no longer cast by actual real people, there is a possibility of dividing a state's electoral votes by fractions. Say the popular vote in our previous example had divided 55% to 45% instead of 60% to 40%. Why not give Candidate B 2.25 electoral votes and Candidate A 2.75 votes? The Popular Electoral Vote Amendment requires that states still cast only whole electoral votes. There are several reasons to keep the electoral vote system still somewhat "chunky" by forbidding fractional votes:

1.   *Whole votes provide a floor for third party candidates.* There are always many third party candidates in presidential elections. In the most recent election they cumulatively received 6% of the national popular vote. In 1992 Ross Perot won 19% of the popular vote. Third parties play an important role in our democracy. They often advance significant positions and issues which the Republican and Democratic parties try to ignore. Yet, in our system of government there is only one president in the end. Our system does not accommodate the often unstable and fractious multi-party coalition governments common in parliamentary systems. How do you balance the need to allow third

parties a voice, while assuring that tiny minorities do not prevent the rest of the Nation from finally picking one person to be president?

The Popular Electoral Vote Amendment achieves this balance by keeping electoral votes whole. This means that, to receive any electoral votes, a third party candidate would have to achieve a high enough vote in a state to equal whatever proportion of a state's popular vote corresponds to a full electoral vote. Going back to the example of our hypothetical state with five electoral votes, this would mean that a third party (or major party) candidate would need to receive at least one-fifth of the state's votes to receive one of its five electoral votes. Thus, third parties with significant support would be represented in the national vote, while truly fringe parties would not be allowed to confuse a nation-wide final decision.

2.   *Whole votes reduce the impact of recounts and election fraud.* In the 2000 presidential race, the reason the recount in Broward County was so critical was that, because of Florida's winner-takes-all law, the recount was going to decide the allocation of all of Florida's 25 electoral votes. If the Popular Electoral Vote Amendment had been in effect at that time, only one electoral vote would have been at stake, not 25, and the entire election would not have turned on one county's recount. However, as noted in the last chapter, if there were a national direct popular vote system, in a close election, every county and precinct would have had to go through the nightmare that Broward County suffered in 2000. A proportional electoral vote system where electoral votes are kept whole balances the two extremes. Fractional votes would drive us toward the nightmare scenario of a nation-wide recount as with a direct popular vote system. However, with whole votes allocated proportionately, only one electoral vote would be in play, much less likely to sway the entire national vote of 538 electoral votes. The same effect would apply to election fraud. With whole electoral votes, election fraud would usually have to affect large

numbers of votes to make any difference. However, the larger the fraud, the more likely it would be to detect.

3. *Whole votes incentivize voters and campaigns to try harder.* One of the objectives of the Popular Electoral Vote Amendment is to encourage presidential candidates to run national campaigns reaching out to all 50 states, not just a few swing states. Another objective is to encourage voters to become engaged in the process, motivated by the knowledge that their participation will help their favored candidate obtain electoral votes even if she or he may not carry their state overall. However, both human being voters, and that special form of human being known as politicians, work harder with goals in view. With a direct popular vote system, any incremental effort would be only marginally rewarded. However, with the election based on proportionally allocated whole electoral votes, a whole new incentive structure is created. Shooting for enough votes to get one more electoral vote is a far more visible and motivating target than getting just a few more popular votes.

What if No One Gets 270 Electoral Votes?

Since the Popular Electoral Vote Amendment allows third parties to get electoral votes if they achieve enough votes in a state to yield a whole electoral vote, there is the possibility that no candidate will receive a majority of the electoral votes (currently 270). That possibility actually exists with the current procedures, which were put in place by the Twelfth Amendment in 1804. In that situation, the President is then elected by the House of Representatives from the top three electoral vote recipients. However, this vote is not an ordinary straight-up vote by the members of the House. Instead, each state's congressional delegation combined has one vote. This procedure has been used only once, in 1824, and resulted in the election of the second-place finisher, John Quincy Adams, over the first-place finisher, Andrew Jackson. Jackson was so upset by this that he founded the modern Democratic Party to support his subsequent successful campaign for president against Adams in 1828.

The Popular Electoral Vote Amendment is trying to move our presidential elections closer to the national popular vote while protecting less populous states. It is also trying to promote a more efficient election process by eliminating 200 year old surplus age like meetings of the Electoral Colleges. Therefore, the Popular Electoral Vote Amendment proposes to streamline the process of electing a President in the event no one gets an electoral vote majority. In that case the election will be decided by both houses of Congress voting together. This will parallel the electoral votes minus the District of Columbia's three votes. Instead of voting by states, each member will have one vote. This will avoid the current situation where Vermont has the same vote as California, which is even more skewed than our current winner-takes-all Electoral College system. The combined houses of Congress will also choose among only the top two electoral vote recipients, and will vote, as is our modern practice, for President and Vice President as a team. (The Twelfth Amendment provides for the Senate to elect the Vice President separately, which raises the possibility of a Vice President being elected from a different party than the President.)

So, How Does this Work? Rerunning 2000

To illustrate how proportional electoral voting would work on the state level, let's look at Utah in the most recent election. The breakdown of the popular vote there was 46% for Trump, 28% for Clinton, and 21% for independent conservative Evan McMullin. The balance went to various small third parties. Under the Popular Electoral Vote Amendment, instead of all six of Utah's electoral votes going to Trump, even though he got less than a majority of the state's popular vote, the six electoral votes would have been allocated three to Trump, two to Clinton and one to McMullin.

It is tempting to rerun national elections to see how this new system would play out. However, cautions are in order. Campaigns are run based on the rules in place. Presidential campaigns run under the current system focus on a few swing states. If there was a direct popular vote system in place, campaigns would focus instead on their sectional strongholds to most efficiently maximize their raw popular vote total. Under a Popular Electoral Vote Amendment system, campaigns would push for votes in all 50 states, and rely heavily on local grassroots activism. Each of these could produce very different outcomes. Furthermore, individual voters would respond differently if they knew that their presidential vote was definitely going to count instead of possibly being zeroed out by a winner-takes-all law.

With that very major caveat, let's review the 2000 election, to see how it would have played out if the Popular Electoral Vote Amendment had been in effect then. We are doing the 2000 election rather than 2016 election because there are still allegations in flux about the results of the most recent election, and claims are still fresh that the campaigns would have been run differently under different rules. Also, with the 2016 election the temptation would be to simply ask if Clinton would have won, or if Trump still would have won, and leave it at that. However, the Popular Electoral Vote Amendment would not be retroactive, and would not change the results of any past election. Our purpose is to come up with rules that make sense for future elections, not to play what-if with the past.

The 2000 election also makes a better test case because it was much closer in terms of both popular and electoral votes than the recent election. We are using the reported popular vote totals. These are still disputed by some, and are based on campaigns run under the Electoral College system rules. The campaigns would certainly have been run differently, and produced different results, had the Popular Electoral Vote Amendment been in effect at the time.

Presidential Election of 2000 under Popular Electoral Vote

State	Gore	Bush	Nader
Alabama	4	5	
Alaska	1	2	
Arizona	4	4	
Arkansas	3	3	
California	29	23	2
Colorado	4	4	
Connecticut	5	3	
Delaware	2	1	
District of Columbia	3	0	
Florida	12	13	
Georgia	6	7	
Hawaii	2	2	
Idaho	1	3	
Illinois	12	10	
Indiana	5	7	
Iowa	4	3	
Kansas	2	4	
Kentucky	3	5	
Louisiana	4	5	
Maine	2	2	
Maryland	6	4	
Massachusetts	8	4	
Michigan	9	9	
Minnesota	5	5	
Mississippi	3	4	

Missouri	5	6	
Montana	1	2	
Nebraska	2	3	
Nevada	2	2	
New Hampshire	2	2	
New Jersey	9	6	
New Mexico	3	2	
New York	20	12	1
North Carolina	6	8	
North Dakota	1	2	
Ohio	10	11	
Oklahoma	3	5	
Oregon	4	3	
Pennsylvania	12	11	
Rhode Island	3	1	
South Carolina	3	5	
South Dakota	1	2	
Tennessee	5	6	
Texas	12	20	
Utah	1	4	
Vermont	2	1	
Virginia	6	7	
Washington	6	5	
West Virginia	2	3	
Wisconsin	6	5	
Wyoming	0	3	
Totals	266	269	3

The bottom line is that, due to Green Party candidate Ralph Nader's three electoral votes, neither Al Gore nor George W. Bush would have received a 270 electoral vote majority. This very close election would have been decided by the houses of Congress voting together. How would the Congress have voted? Like the national presidential vote that year, the Congress elected in 2000 was very narrowly divided. The Republicans held a small three-seat majority in the House, and the Senate was evenly split. And in those ancient times, there were dozens of conservative Democrats and liberal Republicans who represented districts and states carried by the other party's presidential candidate. No one can say how those members of Congress would have voted.

Democrats will be displeased that the Popular Electoral Vote Amendment would not have inevitably led to Al Gore's election. Republicans will be nervous that Gore might have prevailed in a closely divided Congress. However, the 2000 election will never be run again. And if we learned anything from the most recent election, it is that no one can predict what future elections will bring. The goal of the Popular Electoral Vote Amendment is not to promote the election of a Democrat or Republican. Its goal is to put in place sensible procedures acceptable to both parties assuring that, in the future, it will be the United States' citizens who decide who their leaders will be.

We can say one thing with confidence about this rerun of the 2000 election. Whatever the outcome, it would have been decided by people elected by, and accountable to, the American people. Regardless of one's view of the relative merits of the two candidates, no one can dispute that that election was ultimately decided by a one-vote majority of the United States Supreme Court. And regardless of one's view of the Court's decision in the case of *Bush v. Gore*, a large majority of Americans would certainly agree that it is far more democratic that hundreds of democratically elected and accountable legislators make that decision rather than five unelected and unaccountable judges.

THREE

Of Citizens, Subjects and Rotten Boroughs:
The Popular Electoral Vote Amendment Part II

Assuring that every citizen's vote counts requires more than reforming the Electoral College system. Just as citizens can be deprived of their voice by winner-takes-all laws in presidential elections, citizens can also lose their voice by having their voting power diluted. This is what happened under the three-fifths compromise. The votes of citizens in slave states counted more than those of citizens in free states because the slave states' representation in the House of Representatives and their electoral votes in presidential races took into account their non-voting slave populations.

In order to put the three-fifths compromise into effect, the Constitution provides that the allocation of seats in the House of Representatives and Electoral College votes be based on a state's total population, rather than its number of citizens. It was argued that the politicians elected by voting citizens represented and spoke for the interests of the non-voting enslaved population. This absurd argument did not disappear even when slavery was abolished after the Civil War, but redeployed to argue against women's suffrage. Women did not need the vote, it was argued, because their husbands and fathers would represent the women's interests as well as their own when the men voted. With this attitude in control, House seats and Electoral College votes continued to be allocated counting the female half of the population, even though they could not vote.

Happily, with the Fifteenth Amendment in 1870 guaranteeing the vote to former enslaved men, and the Nineteenth Amendment in 1920 extending the vote to all women in the United States (some individual states had given women the vote before then), all adult citizens generally have the right to vote. We should also note the Twenty-sixth Amendment of 1971 guaranteeing the vote to citizens at the age of 18. However, despite these advances in extending the right to vote, an after-effect of the three-fifths compromise continues to diminish most citizens' voting power in favor of a small minority of voters.

The United States' Modern Rotten Boroughs

As noted earlier, the idea that an elected legislature should be the supreme body of government was established in modern times by Britain's Glorious Revolution of 1689. The United States Congress, like the American state legislatures which created the United States, is directly modeled on Britain's Parliament. However, the framers of the United States' Constitution made some important improvements. One of these was to recognize that populations grow and move. Therefore, the Constitution provides for a census every ten years and the re-allocation of seats in the House of Representatives (and consequently electoral votes as well) based on population changes found by the census. Of course, to implement the three-fifths compromise the re-allocation is based on total population rather than voting citizens, but at least there is a method to take into account shifts among the people between and within states.

Britain did not have such a regular re-adjustment. As a result, over time there began to be significant differences in the number of voters represented by different parliamentary seats. Seats with fewer voters were called "rotten boroughs," because the low number of voters made it easy for politicians to get elected in them without having to account much to the country's citizenry. (Eventually, in the 1830s Britain began to re-adjust the boundaries of parliamentary districts to align better with the number of voters in each constituency.)

Astonishingly, 150 years after the end of the slavery that was the basis for three-fifths compromise, it continues to result in modern rotten boroughs in the United States. Instead of pro-slavery politicians counting their slaves to get more power in Congress and presidential elections, these modern rotten boroughs are based on congressional districts with disproportionate numbers of non-citizen residents.

In recent decades, the United States has experienced historically high levels of immigration. The Census Bureau estimates that 7% of the people living in the United States, both legally and illegally, are not citizens. Yet they are counted in allocating congressional seats and electoral votes. The problem is that, like slaves before emancipation, and unlike women before suffrage, these non-citizens are unevenly distributed both throughout the Nation and within states. This can be seen from the following table based on Census Bureau estimates made in 2014.

(Note that the total percentage of non-citizens is certainly much higher than shown in this table, because it is unlikely that most undocumented residents fill out Census forms. However, for purposes of this discussion, these are the numbers that count because the Census numbers determine House seats and electoral votes. Note also that these are estimates, and subject to various margins of error which are given in the Census Bureau reports. These are estimates because the census currently counts total gross population, not citizen population. However, it is quite feasible to count citizens (as well as total residents for informational purposes). In the 2000 and some earlier censuses, the "long-form" census request asked about citizenship status, so the format needed for the Census forms has already been developed and tested. It would be a simple "check-the-box" question. Are you a citizen, and on what basis?)

Percentage of Total State Population who are Citizens

State	Percentage	State	Percentage
California	85.9	Idaho	96.2
Texas	89.1	Oklahoma	96.2
New York	89.5	Alaska	96.7
New Jersey	89.7	Arkansas	96.8
Florida	90.5	South Carolina	96.9
Arizona	91.2	Michigan	96.9
Hawaii	92.2	Indiana	96.9
Maryland	92.5	Tennessee	97.0
Illinois	92.6	Pennsylvania	97.0
Washington	92.8	Iowa	97.1
Connecticut	92.9	Wisconsin	97.3
New Mexico	93.5	New Hampshire	97.4
Rhode Island	93.5	Louisiana	97.6
Massachusetts	93.9	Alabama	97.7
Colorado	93.9	Missouri	97.8
Virginia	94.0	Kentucky	97.8
Oregon	94.0	Wyoming	97.9
Georgia	94.0	Ohio	98.0
Utah	94.6	North Dakota	98.1
North Carolina	94.9	South Dakota	98.2
Delaware	95.5	Vermont	98.2
Kansas	95.6	Maine	98.4
Nevada	95.7	Mississippi	98.5
Nebraska	95.8	Montana	99.0
Minnesota	96.1	West Virginia	99.1

As you can see, there are large differences in the percentage of citizens among the states. Some states have large non-citizen populations while most states have almost none. The result of this after-effect of the three-fifths compromise is modern-day rotten boroughs. Just as slave-owners had more voting power because they got votes for three-fifths of their slaves, the citizens in these modern rotten boroughs have more voting power than other Americans just because they have a lot of non-citizens living near them. Most of these are in California. If seats in the House of Representatives and electoral votes were apportioned based on the states' population of citizens rather than the gross population, even the second and third states on the list, Texas and New York, would probably lose only one House seat and electoral vote each. However, the discrepancy for California would be four or five.

Some may argue that five seats and votes out of 435 is not a significant discrepancy. However, those are House seats and electoral votes that would otherwise belong to other states, states which may strongly care about them. For example, Rhode Island has two House seats, but is at serous risk of losing a seat in the re-apportionment to follow the 2020 census. While we cannot predict the final result of that census, it is more likely that Rhode Island would keep its second seat and corresponding electoral vote if the allocation is based on citizen population rather than gross population.

Nor should this be a partisan issue. While California overall is Democrat, that does not mean that all of the House seats lost as a result of such an adjustment would be Democrat. A significant element of California's non-citizen population are agricultural workers, and their presence creates rotten boroughs in rural Republican areas, just as other immigrant populations cause them in Democrat inner cities. And House seats and votes shifted to other states could result in likely Democrat advantage, such as if Rhode Island holds its second House seat and corresponding electoral vote. Such a shift would also benefit native-born African-Americans, who have very high rates of citizenship and have been reliably Democrat.

This rotten borough effect can be even more pronounced within states. For example, according to the Census Bureau estimates, the overall percentage of New York state residents who are citizens is 89.5%. This means that 10.5% of the residents of New York state are non-citizens. However, the percentage of non-citizens in New York City is much higher. In New York City, non-citizens make up 17.6% of the population, compared to 10.5% in the state as a whole. And if New York City is subtracted from the New York state totals, the difference is even sharper. Outside of New York City, only 5.24% of New York residents are non-citizens.

This has a material impact on the apportionment of the state legislature. As a resident of New York City, I now have about 15% more representation in the state legislature apportioned based on the gross population than I would if the legislature were apportioned based on the citizen population. That translates into New York City having at least 10 rotten borough seats in the 150 member Assembly (the lower house of the New York state legislature). Given the disproportionate financial and media clout that New York City already wields in the state of New York, it strikes me as unfair that New York City residents like me should get extra voting power in the state legislature because of the accident that we have more non-citizen neighbors than other New Yorkers. It's as though, instead of a three-fifths rule, we had a five-sixths rule. New York citizens who live outside of New York City only get five-sixths of the vote of a citizen who lives in New York City.

Similar rotten borough effects exist in many other states where non-citizens are geographically concentrated. Now, in the last chapter we argued that one reason for keeping electoral voting by states is that it gave a little advantage to small, less populous and less influential states based on having two electoral votes corresponding to their two United States Senators. However, this rotten borough effect has the opposite result. Instead of giving a little offset to less powerful states, these modern rotten boroughs generally benefit powerful, white, well-to-do urbanites in our largest and most powerful states.

Due to gerrymandering it is difficult to identify specifically which electoral districts might be affected by a switch to apportioning by citizen rather than gross population. Gerrymandered districts are created by elaborate computer programs which slice and dice communities and census districts, and such an analysis would probably require similar computer processing.[1]

However, the principle stands regardless of the partisan party impact. The vote of American citizens should not be diluted by apportioning federal and state electoral districts on the basis of gross population. Therefore, the Popular Electoral Vote Amendment provides that House seats and electoral votes be allocated on the basis of citizen population, not gross population. Our current practice of apportioning on the basis of gross population is just a carry-over from the three-fifths compromise. In order to effect this change, the Amendment also requires that the census count citizens (although it can continue to count gross population for other purposes, such as the allocation of federal grants).

---

[1]   Gerrymandering refers to where the dominant political party in a state creates often bizarrely shaped districts to maximize the number of seats it holds. It is aptly described as a system where the politicians choose the voters rather then the other way around. Chapter 11 of my book *Timely Renewed: Amendments to Restore the American Constitution*, proposes a constitutional amendment which would eliminate gerrymandering.

Abolish Citizenship?

Federal law and the laws of all 50 states require that one be a United States citizen in order to vote. However, that is not required by the Constitution. Currently the Constitution allows states to set voting requirements. The only restriction is that the same qualifications apply to electors as apply to the larger house of the state legislature. This means that a state could abolish the requirement that one be a citizen in order to vote.

Undoubtedly such a move would be controversial. However, if we continue to allocate House seats and electoral votes on the basis of gross population, then shouldn't the gross population be allowed to vote? Many Americans have always assumed that one should be a citizen in order to vote. However, that assumption is being actively challenged in many parts of the Nation, especially in California.

Most Americans are probably not aware that courts have been striking down restrictions on non-citizens for many years. Courts have ruled that non-citizens can be lawyers (even if in the country illegally) and police officers, serve on juries, and be elected to local office. The requirement that one be a citizen in order to vote may be one of the last remaining features of citizenship. Why not just get rid of the entire concept of citizenship? After all, we are all human beings. Why be so prejudiced against those who are newly arrived in our country?

This argument is, of course, insane. No country on earth allows anyone to vote just because they manage to physically get themselves into the country. It is imminently reasonable for a nation to expect that people show some minimal loyalty and commitment before allowing them to decide who runs the country. Therefore, the Popular Electoral Vote Amendment closes the aforementioned loophole, and requires that one be a citizen in order to vote. Since that is still the law in all 50 states, such a clause should not be controversial.

Clarifying Birthright Citizenship

Affirming in the Constitution that only citizens can vote and be counted in apportioning House seats and electoral votes raises this question: who is a citizen? The Constitution gives Congress the exclusive power to "establish a uniform rule of naturalization." From that follows the power to regulate immigration and, one would think, to define citizenship. However, before the Civil War this was not clear. Therefore, in 1868 the Fourteenth Amendment was enacted. A grab-bag of post-Civil War issues, the first sentence of the first section provides that all "persons born … in the United States and subject to the jurisdiction thereof, are citizens of the United States and of the State wherein they reside." The purpose of the clause was to assure the citizenship of the newly emancipated slaves. However, due to its vague wording, it has been applied beyond that original purpose. [2]

The interpretation of this clause became an issue early in the last election, when Donald Trump questioned whether children born to parents in the United States illegally should have this automatic "birthright citizenship." The major Supreme Court case on the matter, *United States v. Wong Kim Ark* in 1898, did not definitively settle the question. In that case, the Supreme Court ruled that an American born to Chinese parents in California was a citizen. However, although non-citizens, Wong's parents were legally in the United States under the laws in effect when he was born. Therefore, one could argue that the *Wong* case (and the Fourteenth Amendment) does not apply to children born to parents in the United States illegally.

---

[2] Vague wording is a problem with the entire first section of the Fourteenth Amendment, allowing courts license to re-write the Constitution in ways objectionable to both progressives and conservatives. For more on this, see chapter 9 (The Four-Word Constitution) in my book, *Timely Renewed: Amendments to Restore the American Constitution*.

Faced with this argument, defenders of birthright citizenship for babies born to parents in the United States illegally look back to the law preceding the Fourteenth Amendment. Under the old British law, everyone born in lands controlled by the British Crown were *subjects* of his or her Britannic Majesty. Why did the British Empire have such an expansive view of who belonged to it? The answer is simple. Subjects were possessions. They could be taxed and conscripted into the royal military. Subjects could be forced to obey imperial laws and flogged, imprisoned and hung if they did not obey.

What subjects did not have was just as important. Subjects did not have the right to vote. That was an entirely different matter. You had to live in Britain and be a property-owning man to vote for members of Parliament. This rule became a major complaint in the British North American colonies, and later in British domains such as India.

The American and French Revolutions introduced an entirely different concept. This was the *citizen*. Unlike a subject, a citizen has rights as well as responsibilities. Citizens' adherence to their nation is not based on subjugation, but rather on voluntary fidelity. And, citizens can vote. If you do not believe there is a difference, just try telling someone from Britain that they are a British *subject*, and watch them bridle and insist that they are rather a *citizen* of the United Kingdom.

Just as the Popular Electoral Vote Amendment does away with the vestiges of the three-fifths compromise by basing the apportionment of House seats and electoral votes on the citizen population rather than the gross population, it also does away with the last vestiges of the British imperial legal concept of Americans as subjects, as possessions of the government, rather than citizens. This is done by clarifying that only persons born to a parent legally resident in the United States have birthright citizenship. The United States should be ruled only by its citizens, and citizenship should be based on accepting the responsibility of obedience to the laws made by one's fellow citizens. These include the laws governing immigration.

This raises the question of what happens to the millions of children born in the United States to parents who are here in violation of the immigration laws. Obviously, they did not choose to be born here. (Note that this is a different group than so-called "dreamers," persons born in other countries and brought to the United States as children by parents who entered or remained in the United States illegally.) Although children born in the United States to foreign nationals who are in the United States illegally can usually claim citizenship in their parents' home countries, they have been raised here, and thought that they were United States citizens.

The solution here is simple, and within Congress' current power even without a constitutional amendment. These millions should receive an amnesty and a permanent right to residence in the United States, with a pathway to eventual citizenship if they do not have criminal records. It should be enough for advocates of limiting immigration that the Popular Electoral Vote Amendment will make this a closed class. Once the amendment is enacted, children thereafter born in the United States to those who are here illegally will have the same illegal status as their parents.[3] This is the same rule that applies in almost every other

---

[3] This will put to rest the specious argument that deportation breaks up families. Even under current law, children born to foreign nationals illegally in the United States can almost always claim citizenship in their parents' home country. And there never was any law preventing deportees from taking their American-born children with them back to these home countries. Deportation seems harsh, but it is necessary for any nation which is serious about controlling immigration. The Popular Electoral Vote Amendment will definitely make it clear that children born in the U.S. to those here illegally have no claim to U.S. citizenship, so their families can always be deported intact.

nation on earth. Allowing those who relied on the previous confused state of the law to stay is a decent balance with the need to assure that the United States is again ruled by its citizens, as provided by the Popular Electoral Vote Amendment.

You don't like it? Why you should still support the Popular Electoral Vote Amendment

The Popular Electoral Vote Amendment is a compromise. It has aspects that Republicans will like, and that they will dislike, and the same for Democrats. The default for Republicans is to leave the current system in place. For Democrats the temptation is to pursue a hopeless, impossible quest for a pure direct popular vote to elect the President. However, there are major partisan political reasons why it is imperative for both to support the Popular Electoral Vote Amendment. The next two chapters lay out these partisan political imperatives, and explain why it is the political self-interest of both Democrats and Republicans to enact the Amendment.

We start with the Republicans, not to favor them, but because they think they support the status quo. However, they face political doom if they keep the current Electoral College system in place. And, for entirely different reasons, Democrats also face political doom if they do not support the Popular Electoral Vote Amendment.

Note that both of these chapters are written to show the Amendment's partisan advantages to each party. Both are therefore preceded by a trigger warning, as they could be distressful to partisans of the other side, as well as to the short-sighted among the party to which the chapter is addressed.

FOUR

Why Republicans Should Support the Popular Electoral Vote Amendment

TRIGGER WARNING: This chapter may contain information which could be *disturbing, even traumatizing*, to Democrats (and some Republicans).

To date, Republicans have done pretty well by the Electoral College system. They have won all four elections where the winner of the Electoral College vote got fewer popular votes than the Electoral College loser.[4] Faced with new Democrat attacks after Hillary Clinton lost the Electoral Colleges to Donald Trump, despite winning almost three million more votes, Republican writers have leapt to the defense of the Electoral College system. However, these writers are being myopic. In both the long and short term, the winner-takes-all Electoral College system is one of the greatest threats to the Republican Party.

The 'Blue Wall' Is Real, and Survives

The term "blue wall" refers to the fact that, in recent decades, states with a near majority of electoral votes have always voted Democrat in

---

[4] We might also include the defeat of Andrew Jackson by John Quincy Adams in 1824 as a fifth example. Although that race was decided in the House of Representatives and the election preceded the formation of our current political parties, Adams' election was the result of our overall presidential election system, and he did get fewer votes than Jackson. Jackson formed the modern Democratic party as a result of his defeat in that election, and most of Adams' supporters became Republicans when that party was founded a few decades later. Thus, we could retroactively count 1824 as a proto-Republican win and a proto-Democratic defeat.

presidential elections.   Before the most recent election, Democrat presidential candidates could count on starting the race with 242 of the 270 electoral votes needed to win as already "in the bag." While there were also some consistently Republican states, sometimes called the "red hedge," those states have only 102 electoral votes. A Democrat only had to carry a few swing states to win, whereas a Republican had to carry every possible swing state to have any chance of winning.   If we compare the presidential race to a mile run, it is as though the Democrat candidate began every race with a quarter mile head start.

States voting for the same party in all presidential elections 1992 – 2012 (electoral votes as of 2012)

Democrat (the "Blue Wall")		Republican (the "Red Hedge")	
State	Votes	State	Votes
California	55	Alabama	9
Connecticut	7	Alaska	3
District of Columbia	3	Kansas	6
Delaware	3	Idaho	4
Hawaii	4	Mississippi	6
Illinois	20	Nebraska	5
Maine	4	North Dakota	3
Maryland	10	Oklahoma	7
Massachusetts	11	South Carolina	9
Michigan	16	South Dakota	3
Minnesota	10	Texas	38
New Jersey	14	Utah	6
New York	29	Wyoming	3
Oregon	7		
Pennsylvania	20		
Rhode Island	4		
Vermont	3		
Washington	12		
Wisconsin	10		
Totals	242		102

Of course, in the most recent election Donald Trump got past the blue wall by winning Michigan, Pennsylvania and Wisconsin. Those three states' 46 electoral votes supplied Trump's entire Electoral College margin of victory. However, his margin of victory in all of those states was excruciatingly small. He won Pennsylvania and Wisconsin by only 0.008 of the vote, and Michigan by only 0.002 of the vote. Trump won by a combined total of only 77,745 votes out of 13,053,376 votes cast in those states, a margin of only 0.006, or three-fifths of one per cent.

Any small factor could have swung the vote the other way. And one can be certain that the Democrat presidential candidate in 2020 is not going repeat Hillary Clinton's cocky over-confidence and largely ignore Michigan and Wisconsin. Since the election, some Republicans have been wont to boast that Trump "breached," or "collapsed," or "demolished" the blue wall. Such claims are wildly overstated. Donald Trump found a small crack in the blue wall and, with a combination of luck and his unique pluck, managed to squeeze through that little crack. Any Republican who claims that every future Republican presidential candidate can count on repeating Trump's lucky feat, is guilty of the worst political malpractice, or completely delusional. Even Donald Trump, by his own account, was unsure he was going to win.

The blue wall still stands. The blue wall states still strongly tend Democrat in presidential elections, as demonstrated by Trump's agonizingly tiny margins of victory even against the most unpopular Democrat presidential candidate in our times. For Republicans to continue to be competitive in presidential elections, they need to analyze the blue wall systematically, rather than count on lucky cracks to squeeze through it.

Trapped Behind the Blue Wall

The blue wall is entirely an artifact of the winner-takes-all Electoral College system. There are many Republican voters in the blue wall states. However, the winner-takes-all laws permit persistent, but often quite small, Democrat majorities to override all of those Republican votes, and effectively turn them into Democrat votes in the national totals. The following chart illustrates the impact of this phenomenon by showing how many votes Mitt Romney received in the 2012 election in the blue wall states, and how many electoral votes they would have yielded if the Popular Electoral Vote Amendment had been in effect.

Republican Votes Behind the Blue Wall in 2012

State	GOP Vote	WTA Votes* (to Obama)	PEVA Votes* (to Romney)
California	4,839,958	55	20
Connecticut	634,892	7	3
District of Columbia	21381	3	0
Delaware	165,484	3	1
Hawaii	121,015	4	1
Illinois	2,135,216	20	8
Maine	292,276	4	2
Maryland	971,869	10	4
Massachusetts	1,188,314	11	4
Michigan	2,115,256	16	9
Minnesota	1,320,225	10	4
New Jersey	1,477,568	14	7
New York	2,490,431	29	10
Oregon	754,175	7	3
Pennsylvania	2,680,434	20	9
Rhode Island	157,204	4	1
Vermont	92,698	3	1
Washington	1,290,670	12	5
Wisconsin	1,407,966	10	5
Totals	24,157,032	242	97

* WTA = winner-takes-all; PEVA = Popular Electoral Vote Amendment

Over 24 million votes were cast for Mitt Romney in blue wall states in 2012. If the Popular Electoral Vote Amendment had been effect then, Romney would have received 97 electoral votes, representing 40% of all the electoral votes cast by the blue wall states. (In comparison, Donald Trump's electoral vote gain under winner-takes-all from his three blue wall state victories was 46 electoral votes.)

Of course, if the Popular Electoral Vote Amendment were in effect, the Democrat candidate would pick up electoral votes in the red hedge states. To analyze the impact this would have, let's look at a comparable table from 2012 for the red hedge states.

Democratic Votes Behind the Red Hedge in 2012

State	Dem Vote	WTA Votes* (to Romney)	PEVA Votes* (to Obama)
Alabama	795,696	9	3
Alaska	122,640	3	1
Idaho	212,787	4	1
Kansas	440,726	6	2
Mississippi	562,949	6	3
Nebraska	302,081	5	2
North Dakota	124,827	3	1
Oklahoma	443,547	7	2
South Carolina	865,941	9	4
South Dakota	145,039	3	1
Texas	3,308,124	38	16
Utah	251,813	6	1
Wyoming	69,286	3	0
Totals	7,645,456	102	37

* WTA = winner-takes-all; PEVA = Popular Electoral Vote Amendment

Thus, even after subtracting the 37 electoral votes Obama would have received from the red hedge states in 2012, the Popular Electoral Vote Amendment would have netted Romney 60 more electoral votes compared to what he received under the existing winner-takes-all rules. This is still more than the 46 electoral votes Donald Trump gained under winner-takes-all by winning three blue wall states.

The Popular Electoral Vote Amendment would not have won the 2012 election for Mitt Romney. Obama's victory margin of 51% to 47% in the popular vote was too large. What this exercise illustrates is how the Popular Electoral Vote Amendment neutralizes the blue wall phenomenon created by winner-takes-all laws. In a closer election, those net 60 electoral votes could make all the difference, because the blue wall phenomenon makes it entirely possible for a Democrat to lose the popular vote but win the Electoral College vote.

Indeed, after the 2012 election, pollster Nate Silver calculated that, due to the blue wall, Romney might have had to win the popular vote by as much as 53% to win the Electoral Colleges. (Silver has since become less firm on the blue wall effect, but the numbers remain.) It has not happened yet but, due to the blue wall, the arithmetic is there. Indeed, the Trump campaign strategized for such a possibility. And we can confidently predict that, as much as Democrats protest the Electoral College system today, they would willingly accept such a victory when it occurs. The Popular Electoral Vote Amendment is the systemic defense against such an event.

Beyond strategic political calculations, there is a major human dimension to Republican support for the Popular Electoral Vote Amendment. One of the proudest moments of the modern Republican Party was its united support for Ronald Reagan's firm stand against Communist rule, a stand for which he was vociferously attacked by Democrat appeasers. One of the key aspects of this stand was defense of the human rights of peoples trapped behind the Iron

Curtain. Now, this is not to suggest that the rights of Republicans in leftist California are being suppressed to the same degree as those of republicans in Communist Poland, but there can be an analogy. The winner-takes-all laws have created a blue wall which has made the votes of 24 million or more Republican believers in limited constitutional government as meaningless as the votes of the Eastern Europeans who wanted democratic republican government before Ronald Reagan set in motion the policies that brought down the Iron Curtain. The modern Republican Party has a duty to those tens of millions of Republicans behind the blue wall to tear down that wall, and make their presidential votes mean something.

Further, who knows how many more Republican votes there will be if Republicans in blue wall states know that their votes will count? While any measurement of the effect of proportionally allocating electoral votes is necessarily speculative, one has to assume that Republican-inclined voters will be more motivated to vote if they know that their votes will produce some electoral votes for the GOP nominee, than when they know that it is effectively impossible for that nominee to carry their state under winner-takes-all.

Valuing Citizenship

All Republicans know that Democrats favor lax or no enforcement of border security and the immigration laws because they are seeking to flood the Nation with poor low-skilled migrants who will vote Democrat. This also satisfies the demand by Democrats' big business patrons for cheap labor to keep the wages of Americans low. (Contrary to Democrat propaganda, big business today favors, and controls, the Democratic Party, not the Republican. After the success of the Tea Party movement, the Republican Party is now far more opposed to corporate welfare and cronyism that the Clinton-Obama run Democrats.)

The Popular Electoral Vote Amendment is no substitute for strong border security or sensible and enforced immigration laws. However, it does enforce some principles which are very important to Republicans. By placing the requirement that only citizens can vote in the Constitution, the Popular Electoral Vote Amendment reinforces the idea that citizenship means something. Republicans believe that citizenship carries responsibilities as well as privileges. Citizens are not free-loaders, collecting the benefits of living in a free Nation without contributing to its support and defense. Republics can only endure when their citizens accept the responsibilities of citizenship, and only those willing to accept those responsibilities should choose a republic's leaders.

One of those responsibilities is obedience to the Republic's laws. That someone who, in flagrant and blatant violation of the Nation's laws, managed to get themselves physically into its territory is thereby entitled to vote, and have their children receive automatic full citizenship, renders the concept of citizenship meaningless. It also is an insult and injustice to all the worthy and worthwhile immigrants who struggle to come to our Nation in compliance with our laws.

Republicans know about Democrat schemes to grant mass amnesty and citizenship to tens of millions of poor, low-skilled aliens here illegally. They are probably less aware that, impatient with the pace at which this scheme to dilute the votes of American citizens is progressing, many Democrats are now scheming to give the vote to non-citizens right away so that Democrats can take power even faster. Statutory defenses against these plans may be inadequate. While necessary, laws and law enforcement cannot stop states from making non-citizens into voters, or making the babies of aliens here illegally into citizens. Only the constitutional clarifications of the Popular Electoral Vote Amendment will enable Republicans to preserve the right of America's citizens to govern our Nation.

FIVE

Why Democrats Should Support the
Popular Electoral Vote Amendment

TRIGGER WARNING: This chapter may contain information which could be *disturbing, even traumatizing,* to Republicans (and some Democrats). Republicans are particularly warned *not* to read the beginning of the second paragraph.

Democrats generally favor election of the President by direct, nation-wide popular vote. Why should they support a proposal which, while aligning our electoral system more closely with the popular vote, still falls short by preserving a small electoral offset for the citizens of less populous and less powerful states, especially when it includes further provisions to appease Republicans such as limiting voting to citizens and restricting birthright citizenship? Why should Democrats have to bargain with the Republicans to buy democracy?

The short answer is this: President Al Gore. President Hillary Clinton. Now, as we saw in the rerun of the 2000 election in Chapter 2, the Popular Electoral Vote Amendment may not automatically result in the election of someone who wins the popular vote by a razor-thin margin. Indeed, if the 2016 campaigns had been run the same as with the Electoral College system, under the Popular Electoral Vote Amendment the large third party vote may have sent that race to Congress as well. However, under the Popular Electoral Vote Amendment races would be run nationally rather than only in swing states, and it will be much less likely that different candidates will win the popular and electoral votes. And if extremely close races do not lead to an electoral vote majority, they will be decided by elected legislators answerable to the People, not by life-tenured judges.

As Donald Trump's presidency moves forward, Democrats recognize, as they may never had before, the awesome power held by the President of the United States, for ill as well as good. The question for Democrats is this. Is it more important for Democrats to pursue the unobtainable goal of direct popular election of the President, or a realistic compromise which moves our elections much closer to the democratic ideal of one person, one vote? The hard facts are that amending the Constitution requires super-majorities. This means Republican support, and Republicans are never going to support direct popular election. The only reform of our presidential election system which has any chance is one which gives Republicans as well as Democrats something they want. That's how compromise works. That's how our government is supposed to work.

It is tempting for Democrats to reject the need to make any concessions to Republicans in this area. Trump's election was a fluke, they argue, a last hurrah of a fast disappearing old white America. However, a closer analysis of historical voting patterns suggests a less sanguine view. As we have noted, this century is not the first time Democratic presidential candidates have won the popular vote but lost the Electoral Colleges. And we could be seeing in our times a repeat of the same patterns which kept Democrats out of the White House for most of over seven decades.

The Solid Coasts – Repeating the Solid South All Over Again?

Of the 18 four-year presidential terms between 1860 and 1932, Democrats occupied the White House for only four. And two of those, the presidency of Woodrow Wilson, were accidents. All historians agree that Wilson only won in 1912 because Theodore Roosevelt ran as a third party candidate and split the usual Republican majority. And most agree that Wilson was re-elected in 1916 by an extremely narrow margin only because of blunders of political strategy by his Republican opponent.

Yet, throughout those 72 years, the Democratic Party was strong. It had great leaders. This was the era of William Jennings Bryan, the great populist champion (and three-time Democratic presidential candidate). Franklin Roosevelt was the Democratic vice-presidential nominee in 1920, and Al Smith became the first Catholic presidential nominee of a major party in 1928. And it almost always got lots of votes. Indeed, it was during this period that Democratic presidential candidates twice won the popular vote while losing the Electoral College vote (1876 and 1888). The strength of the Democratic popular vote in comparison to its Electoral College results can be seen here:

Democratic Presidential Popular vs. Electoral Vote 1860 - 1928

Year	Republican Candidate(s)	Democratic Candidate(s)	Democratic popular %	Democratic electoral %
1860	Lincoln	Douglas/ Breckinridge	47.6	27.7
1864	Lincoln	McClellan	45.0	9.0
1868	Grant	Seymour	47.3	27.2
1872	Grant	Greeley	43.8	18.8
1876	Hayes	Tilden	50.9	49.9
1880	Garfield	Hancock	48.3	42.0
1884	Blaine	Cleveland	48.9	54.6
1888	Harrison	Cleveland	48.6	41.9
1892	Harrison	Cleveland	46.0	62.3
1896	McKinley	Bryan	46.7	39.4
1900	McKinley	Bryan	45.5	34.7
1904	Roosevelt	Parker	37.6	29.4
1908	Taft	Bryan	43.0	33.5
1912	Taft/Roosevelt	Wilson	41.8	81.9
1916	Hughes	Wilson	49.2	52.2
1920	Harding	Cox	34.2	23.9
1924	Coolidge	Davis	28.8	25.6
1928	Hoover	Smith	40.8	16.3

Not only did the Electoral College system constantly undercount the Democratic popular vote, but the two times the Electoral College system worked strongly in favor of Democrats (1892 and 1912 when the Republican vote was split by strong third party candidates), the Electoral College system still wildly distorted the popular vote results. Wilson winning 82% of the electoral votes in 1912 with only 42% of the popular vote should be as objectionable to direct popular election proponents as the 14 Republican victories which swung the other way.

So, why was this grand, dynamic, popular party consistently shut out of the White House for decade after decade? Of course, there were many factors at play over this long period, which represents a third of our national history. However, from the perspective of electoral arithmetic, the Democrats' main problem was simply this: their votes were too geographically concentrated.

In this period white southerners were a core constituency of the Democratic Party. The Democrats so consistently carried the South that it came to be referred to as the "Solid South." Just how solidly Democrat the southern states were is illustrated by the election of 1904.

One of the most popular U. S. presidents is Theodore Roosevelt. And his popularity is not just a recent development. Young, ebullient and dynamic, he was very popular in his own time as well. Having succeeded to the presidency upon the assassination of William McKinley in 1901, T. R. was running for a full term at the head of the ticket in 1904. Having lost two elections in a row with William Jennings Bryan (who, although the analogy is not perfect, might be thought of as the Bernie Sanders of his time), in 1904 the Democratic Party turned to a distinguished but obscure New York state judge named Alton B. Parker. The 1904 election has some interesting parallels to the 2016 election. For example, both major party candidates were from New York, and third parties were active, receiving 6% of the vote in both elections.

However, the outcome was very different. Roosevelt won by a landslide, beating Parker in the popular vote 56% to 38% and sweeping the Electoral College votes in every state of the North, Midwest and West. However, the Democrat still carried the South, and by substantial margins. Although most southerners probably knew little about Judge Parker, he still carried South Carolina with 95% of the popular vote, Mississippi with 91% of the popular vote, and Louisiana with 89% of the popular vote. The popular vote margins were also substantial in the other former Confederate states. (A major caveat to these margins is that, by this time, Jim Crow laws were well-established and few southern blacks were allowed to vote.)

However, under winner-takes-all, these popular vote margins in the South were meaningless. One can win all of a state's electoral votes with 46% of the popular vote (as Trump did in Utah and Clinton did in Minnesota in 2016) as well as with 95% (as Parker did in South Carolina in 1904). Winning California by 30 percentage points, Hawaii by 32 and Washington state by 16, or Massachusetts by 27 percentage points, Maryland by 26 and New York by 22, all did not yield Hillary Clinton a single additional electoral vote. As noted in Chapter 1, Clinton's entire popular vote margin can be attributed to her four million vote margin of victory in California, but it made no difference in the Electoral College result. Under winner-takes-all, she would have won all of California's electoral votes even if her margin of victory had been one vote. However, if only a tenth of those extra millions of California votes had found their way to the Midwest, the outcome of the election could have been entirely changed. As is, under winner-takes-all those big Democratic margins are effectively wasted votes.

The negative electoral consequences of this concentration of Democratic votes in the coastal states of the Pacific and Northeast were seen even before the 2016 presidential election. In 2012, Democratic candidates for the House of Representatives received over a million more votes than the Republican candidates, but only 46% of the seats. In 2016, Republican candidates managed to do slightly better than Democrats, receiving 48.7% of the vote to Democrats' 47.9%, but that translated into Republicans holding 55.4% of the seats.

This concentration of Democratic votes can also be seen in the margins of victory in these races. According to the website ballotpedia, in 2012 the average margin of victory for Democratic winners in House elections was 35.7%, while the average for Republicans was only 28.6%. Again in 2016, on average Republicans won by significantly smaller margins than Democrats. The average margin of victory for Democrats was 41.54%, while for Republicans it was only 33.51%.

While it is nice to see Democrats win by large margins when they win, these margins mean that more Democratic voters are in districts which will elect a Democrat in any case, while the more widely spread out Republican voters carry more marginal districts. We now see that this structural problem of concentration of Democratic voters can carry over to presidential as well as congressional races. In analyzing the results of the 2016 election in an interview on NPR, President Obama noted this fundamental structural issue:

> So I think we have a scrambled political landscape right now. There are some things that we know are a challenge for Democrats — structural problems. For example, population distribution, oftentimes younger voters, minority voters, Democratic voters, are clustered in urban areas ... and on the coasts, and so as a consequence you've got a situation where there're not only entire states but also big chunks of states where, if we're not showing up, if we're not in there making an argument, then we're going to lose. And we can lose badly, and that's what happened in this election.

Unlike President Obama, who is one of the most astute and successful Democratic politicians of our time, many Democrats prefer to ignore this issue, and instead blame Republican gerrymandering. While Republican gerrymandering certainly has played a role, like President Obama, most analysts agree that the concentrated distribution of Democratic voters is a far bigger factor in this decade's run of Democratic losses. After all, the Republican take-over of the House in 2010 was before this decade's redistricting, and gerrymandering is irrelevant to Donald Trump's victory.

By aligning the electoral vote more closely with the popular vote, the Popular Electoral Vote Amendment can help obviate the impact of this concentration of Democratic voters in urban areas and coastal states. While Democrats would prefer direct popular election of the President, that is not an option without substantial Republican support, and that is not going to happen. However, the Popular Electoral Vote Amendment can draw the necessary Republican support, and move the United States closer to allowing the people to decide who will lead us.

Depending on Demographic Destiny

Democrats do have hope in the long term future. Every year the proportion of our Nation's population who are of minority groups grows larger. The Census Bureau projects that by 2050 a majority of Americans will be non-white. Further, inspired by Barack Obama's presidency, a large majority of American young people of all ethnic backgrounds believe in the Democratic Party's message of progress and inclusion. It is inevitable as a matter of demography that the Democratic Party will eventually become America's permanent majority party. Why accept a half step of progress like the Popular Electoral Vote Amendment when there will come a time when Democrats will not need Republican votes to enact direct popular election of the President?

Why wait? Republicans have shown that they are willing to nominate and support a presidential candidate who is unqualified, temperamentally unsuited, and disrespectful of America's diverse peoples. They are willing to do that *now*. Can Democrats justify holding out for direct popular election in some distant future, when the current winner-takes-all Electoral College system is producing Donald Trump in the real-time present?

This dependence on demographic destiny risks making Democrats dangerously complacent. Can we wait until 2030 to *begin* seriously addressing climate change? How many millions will die if we wait until 2040 to *begin* providing healthcare for all? What will America become if we are only able to *begin* building a truly inclusive society in 2050?

Something must be done *now*. The Popular Electoral Vote Amendment is a compromise, and contains some features more attractive to Republicans than Democrats. But it would represent a significant movement toward the end goal of giving the people power over their government, and making that government work in the interests of the people rather than the corporations. It is a move which we must take sooner, rather than a later which may be too late.

SIX

Amend the Constitution? Are You Serious?

The Popular Electoral Vote Amendment is an amendment to the United States Constitution. If you are under the age of 50, you cannot remember the last time the Constitution was regularly amended. (It was the 26th Amendment in 1971, guaranteeing the vote to 18 year olds.[5]) And you would have to be over the age of 100 to have any chance of remembering the last time a major national issue was decided by the amendment process. (That was the 19th Amendment in 1920, which extended the vote to all women.)

Most Americans have never seen our Constitution amended because it is the most difficult in the world to amend. The amendment procedures set forth in Article V require that amendments be initiated by two-thirds vote in both houses of Congress followed by ratification by three-fourths of the states.[6] Leaving aside the Bill of Rights amendments (the first 10 amendments) which were enacted almost immediately after the Constitution, our Constitution has been amended only 17 times in 225 years. None of our states or any other democratic nation have amendment thresholds as high as those in Article V.

This was not what the framers of the Constitution intended. They fully expected that there would be regular amendments to the Constitution. After all, the founding generation amended the Constitution 12 times

---

[5]   The 27th Amendment was finally enacted in 1992, but that was an odd measure that was originally proposed in 1791 as part of the Bill of Rights, and did not attract any significant notice when it was finally ratified.

[6]   Constitutional amendments can also be initiated by a convention called by two thirds of the states. However, that has never happened in our Nation's history, and is thus even more useless than initiation by Congress.

within its first two decades. George Washington, for example, thought Article V was the Constitution's most important feature.

The reason the amendment thresholds were set so impossibly high is simply that our Constitution was the first written national constitution in modern history. Its framers had nothing to compare it to. They had no way of knowing that experience would show that the thresholds were too high, and that every other democratic nation and American state would set them lower.

(I have drafted a reform of Article V which would move our constitutional amendment process from being effectively impossible to just very difficult. It would allow states to initiate amendments without having to meet in a convention, and reduce the ratification thresholds slightly. You can read about this proposal, which is called the "Amendment Amendment" in my short book *Are We the People? How We the People Can Take Charge of Our Constitution*.)

Short of reforming the amendment requirements, we are stuck with Article V's high requirements. Is there another way? And is there any realistic possibility that the Popular Electoral Vote Amendment can become part of our Constitution?

Popular Vote Interstate Compact – No Compromise, No Chance

To analyze these questions, it is useful to look at the current leading contender to replace the winner-takes-all Electoral College system. The National Popular Vote Interstate Compact (NPVIC) seeks to circumvent the constitutional amendment process by simply having states with a majority of electoral votes agree to vote for the winner of the national popular vote. A state's electoral votes would go to the winner of the national popular vote even if the other candidate carried that state. So far ten states and the District of Columbia, representing 165 electoral votes, have agreed to this plan. It would go into effect when states with 270 electoral votes sign on.

The NPVIC faces several challenges. The first is that it is probably unconstitutional. Section 10 of Article I of the Constitution provides that no state can "enter into any Agreement or Compact with another State" without the consent of Congress. Nonetheless, supporters of the NPVIC claim it does not need the consent of Congress. The reasoning for this is quite convoluted and unconvincing (unsurprisingly law professors were involved in concocting the scheme). Rather than go into these complicated arguments, for our purposes the important point is that the NPVIC would certainly be challenged in court in any presidential election where it made a difference, which is one where the winner of the popular vote lost the Electoral College vote. Thus, ironically, a proposal which was intended to avoid a repeat of the 2000 election, which was ultimately decided by the Supreme Court, would end up producing the same result, a presidential election decided by the Supreme Court.

Further, even before it was struck down by the Supreme Court, the NPVIC would likely collapse because it is completely unrealistic from a practical political point of view. Any state which was carried by the Electoral College victor would certainly pull out of the NPVIC rather than allow its electoral votes go to the candidate rejected by that state's voters. As an abstract proposition, it is easy to say that states entering into the NPVIC would nobly surrender their electoral votes to the candidate who won in other states. However, let us do a reality check on this by imagining what would have happened if the NPVIC had been in place in the most recent election. (Remembering that many thought the election might have gone the other way. If the blue wall of Democrat states had held but Trump gained only a few more votes in each precinct nationally, he might have won the popular vote but lost the Electoral College vote.)

Democrats regard Donald Trump as a corrupt, perhaps criminally corrupt, disgrace, emotionally volatile and brought into the presidency by racism and the intervention of foreign powers. Republicans regard Hillary Clinton as a definitely criminally corrupt, self-serving tool of coastal elites who hate America. Both regarded the other's candidate as dangerous, a threat to our Nation. In light of Democrats' reaction to

Trump's victory, how would the Democratic majority of states carried by Hillary Clinton have reacted if the NPVIC required them to cast their electoral votes for Donald Trump? Can anyone doubt that there would have been a massive outcry to bust the NPVIC and restore the venerable Electoral College system that would save America from Donald Trump? And would not have Republicans reacted the same to a Hillary Clinton victory, where the Electoral College votes of solidly Republican states were to be cast for that corrupt law-breaker? No, it's one thing to be out-voted by other states. But to be forced to cast one's own state's electoral votes for a dangerous, corrupt candidate rejected by one's own state's voters would not be tolerated.

However, neither a Supreme Court rejection nor a post-election disavowal of the NPVIC are likely outcomes, and for a simple reason. The NPVIC will never be approved by states with the 270 vote majority of the Electoral Colleges. In all of the states which have signed on to the NPVIC, the approval has come from Democratic governors and legislatures. Pollster Nate Silver points out that the eleven jurisdictions which have approved the NPVIC to date were all won by Barack Obama by more than 15 percentage points in 2012. Approval of the NPVIC has stalled, with no new states signing on since 2014, for the simple reason that there are almost no Democrat-controlled states left which have not yet approved the NPVIC. As Silver points out, "until some purple states and red states sign on, the compact has little in the way of territory to conquer."

The NPVIC is a Democrat idea promoted by Democrats to achieve the Democrat goal of direct popular election of the President while avoiding the super-majority requirements of the constitutional amendment process - and Republicans know it. The NPVIC offers nothing to Republicans, and will fail as a result. Perhaps that should not be, but that is political reality. A reform as significant as how we select our President is only going to come about if it offers real benefits to both Democrats and Republicans. As much as both parties have renounced compromise in recent times, our electoral system can only be reformed by a bipartisan approach.

Is Anyone for a Deal?

Obviously, for Democrats, Republican disinterest in the NPVIC is just another example of the GOP's perfidious rejection of democracy. For Republicans, the NPVIC is another example of Democrats' disrespect for federalism and the role of the states as a counter-balance to all-pervasive domination by the federal government.

Recently we seem to have forgotten the arts of compromise and negotiation. They are not about convincing the other side that they are wrong. They are about giving some points in which you believe in order to get some other things that you feel are more important. No deal is a good deal unless all sides are somewhat dissatisfied. A deal is a good deal if both sides feel they have come out well overall, not totally and utterly triumphed over the other side.

The Popular Electoral Vote Amendment is such a deal. Like all deals, it is also a gamble. Will the blue wall of Democrat states with a near-majority of electoral votes snap back into place after Donald Trump's lucky breach, blocking any further Republican presidential wins? Or will it continue to erode, leaving the Democratic vote geographically concentrated in the Solid Coasts, where it will have no more impact than the Solid South did in stopping a new run of decades of Republican domination of the presidency? Today no one can predict which scenario is more probable. However, we can say that either would be the artifact of our current winner-takes-all Electoral College system. Considering the stakes, the safest path for both parties is to act now to eliminate that system, even if that requires some compromise.

Beyond the fate of political parties, all Americans deserve a better national election system. They deserve a system where the votes of all citizens count, not just those in swing states. They deserve a system which provides a little protection for the citizens of less powerful small states, while eliminating rotten borough advantages for more powerful big states. They deserve an electoral system in which our Nation's citizens decide who will lead us. All Americans deserve the Popular Electoral Vote Amendment, *now*.

APPENDIX

Text of the Popular Electoral Vote Amendment

Section 1: For the purpose of electing the President and Vice President, each State shall be entitled to a number of Electoral Votes equal to the whole number of Senators and Representatives to which the State may be entitled in the Congress. In each election, each State shall allocate its Electoral Votes in proportion to the vote in that State received by each pair of candidates for President and Vice President, but no partial Electoral Votes shall be allocated, nor shall any candidates receive an Electoral Vote where the proportion of the vote they receive is less than that proportion which would correspond to one whole Electoral Vote in that State in that election. States must cast each Electoral Vote for a combined pair of candidates for President and Vice President who shall have consented to the joining of their names as candidates for the offices of President and Vice President.

Section 2: Each State will transmit a sealed and certified copy of its allocation of Electoral Votes to the Speaker of the House of Representatives so as to be received no later than the fourth day of January next following the election, or on such other day as Congress may appoint. The Speaker of the House of Representatives shall, in the presence of the Senate and House of Representatives, open all the certificates and the Electoral Votes shall then be counted. Any pair of persons having a majority of Electoral Votes for President and Vice President shall be declared the President and Vice President. If no pair of President and Vice President candidates receives a majority of Electoral Votes, the Senators and Representatives then present shall proceed immediately to elect a President and Vice President from among the two pairs of candidates who shall have received the most Electoral Votes. In this election, each Senator and Representative shall have one vote, and the pair of candidates who receives the most votes shall be elected President and Vice President.

Section 3: Neither the United States nor any State shall permit to vote, or count the vote of, any person who is not a citizen of the United States in any election for any office which is empowered to make or enforce laws. Citizenship of the United States shall be as determined by Congress, subject to the first sentence of the first section of the fourteenth amendment to this Constitution, except that said sentence shall be deemed clarified as of the day after its enactment to provide that a person born in the United States shall not be a citizen of the United States unless (a) one parent of the person is a citizen of the United States; (b) one parent of the person is an alien lawfully admitted for permanent residence in the United States who resides in the United States; (c) one parent of the person is an alien performing active service in the Armed Forces of the United States; or (d) the person is naturalized in accordance with the laws of the United States.

Section 4: The apportionment of Representatives among the several States and the membership of all States' legislatures shall be according to the number of citizens resident in each State and each State electoral district as of each decennial Enumeration. Such Enumerations shall report the numbers of citizens as needed for such apportionments as well as such other information as Congress shall prescribe.

Section 5: The Congress shall have the power to enforce this article by appropriate legislation.

Made in the USA
San Bernardino, CA
28 June 2018